Christmas
Programs
for Children

compiled by

Pat Fittro

S ™
STANDARD
PUBLISHING
Cincinnati. Ohio

The Standard Publishing Company, Cincinnati, Ohio
A division of Standex International Corporation
© 1995 by The Standard Publishing Company

ISBN 0-7847-0380-9

Contents

To All of You

Helen Kitchell Evans

I want to bring a greeting
To all of you today,
A special Christmas greeting
So I have this to say:
It's because Jesus came to earth
That we celebrate each year His
birth.

Christmas News

Iris Gray Dowling

The angels carried Heaven's news
To lonely shepherds Christmas
Eve.
Who left their sheep out in the
fields,
Because God's message they
believed.

Jesus Is Born

Iris Gray Dowling

Hear the church bells ring—
Early Christmas morn.
Hear the choir sing—
Jesus Christ is born.

*(Introduce with organ chimes and
follow this rhyme with the choir
singing a carol.)*

Rejoicing for the Boy

Helen Kitchell Evans

Joy! Joy! Joy!
The baby Jesus came.
Heaven's precious Boy!
Oh, praise His matchless name!

Joy! Joy! Joy!
The Savior entered in.
Sinless perfect Boy
To save the world from sin.

Thank You!

Dixie Phillips

When I think of Jesus' birthday,
It makes me want to say:
"Thank You for coming to earth for
me.
"Thank You for dying to set me
free."
When I think of His humble birth,
How He left Heaven to come to
this earth.
I just have to say:
"Thank You Jesus, and happy
birthday!"

Well—Merry Christmas

Helen Kitchell Evans

You have to be real brave
To face a crowd this way.
And stand up tall and remember
What you are going to say.
(Pause.)
Let's see—
Well, HAPPY CHRISTMAS.
(Leaves hurriedly.)

Christmas Action Poem

Dixie Phillips

Let us see the baby, *(Hand above eyes.)*
Lying on the hay. *(Fold hands and rest them on face.)*
It is baby Jesus
Born this Christmas Day. *(Rock arms as if holding baby.)*

Wise men came to see Him, *(Children march.)*
Shepherds did too. *(Crook arm like staff.)*
I love Him with all my heart. (Cross arms over chest.)
Do you and you and YOU? *(Point to others.)*

Shining Christmas Star

Dixie Phillips

Oh shining Christmas star that shines so bright.
Shine down on mankind tonight.
We need Your love. We need Your care.
We need to know that You are there.
Our world is dark and growing dim,
Please come and guide mankind to Him.
He—Who can change the heart of man.
He—Who extends to us His hand.
Oh shining Christmas star that shines so bright.
Shine down on mankind tonight.

An Honor

Dixie Phillips

My mommy said it was an honor to say my piece up here.
She said that it would bring a lot of joy and cheer.
So here I go with all my might:
(Cup hands around mouth.)
"Baby Jesus was born one holy night!"
I think I've done my very best.
Please clap if you think I passed the test!
(Boy—bow, Girl—curtsy.)

What Matters

Helen Kitchell Evans

What day did Jesus come to earth?
What day did Mary give Him birth?
Scholars quite often disagree
But no matter the day, He came for me.

No matter where His tiny head lay,
On a pillow or sweet smelling hay;
No matter the shepherds who came to see,
No matter the wise men, He came for me.

No matter that angels sang on high,
No matter the star in the midnight sky;
What matters is only He came, you see,
To live, to teach and to die for me.

Why We Speak

Cora M. Owen

Christmas verses we recite,
Celebrating holy night!
Making us again rejoice,
Praising God with heart and voice.

We're so glad that Jesus came;
So we speak in His dear name;
Bidding everyone believe,
Christ of Christmas to receive.

Join and Stay

Helen Kitchell Evans

I'm not bothered one bit
To stand up here this way;
I'm not bothered one bit
So hear what I have to say;

All of you are welcome,
And if you are visiting today
Won't you come again.
Please join us and stay.

Christmas in Your Heart

Kay Hoffman

It will always seem like Christmas
    What e'er the time of year,
When you do a kindly deed,
    Give away a word of cheer.

The shops are filled with fancy gifts
    To give when Yule bells chime,
But heart-gifts that we give away
    Require no special time.

Reach out a hand to help
    someone,
    Cheer some heart today,
The world needs love and caring
    On each and every day.

Though Yuletide scenes may
    disappear
    And no longer play the part,
It will always seem like Christmas
    When it's Christmas in your heart!

Christmas Prayer

Alyce Pickett

Last night I prayed to Jesus
    Just like I always do,
But, since it was Christmas Eve,
    I said some extras, too.

I prayed for all poor folk to have
    At least some kind of toy
To give their children Christmas
    Day,
    Each little girl and boy.

I asked for children everywhere
    To have good food next day,
And that not one would be
    crippled,
    Or feel too sick to play.

Then I told Jesus, "I am glad
    You'll know just what to do
So the children will be happy,
    And know You love them, too."

7

We Love Him

Lillian Robbins

Christmas is a special time
  For presents and toys and cake.
But mother says that's not the reason
  We always celebrate.

It's all because Jesus came
  Born in Bethlehem.
We know He loves us very much,
  And all of us love Him.

How I Love to Hear It

Cora M. Owen

How I love to hear the tale
Of Christmas long ago.
It is told in God's own word.
That's how I know it's so.

How I love to think about
That little Babe so fair,
Lying in a manger bed.
The Son of God was there.

How I love to hear about
The angels' holy song;
Singing words with praises sweet,
That to the Lord belong.

How I love to read about
When shepherds heard the news;
How they hastened to His side.
They came, no time to lose.

I'm Glad I'm Me

Orpha A. Thomas

If I were a doggie, I'd bark.
  (Child says "woof, woof.")

If I were a kitty I'd meow.
  (Child says "meow, meow.")

If I were a lamb, I'd say baa.
  (Child says "baa, baa.")

If I were a pigeon, I'd coo.
  (Child says "coo, coo.")

I'm glad that I'm a little child
On this bright Christmas Day.

I can tell Jesus I love Him
When I kneel down to pray.
(Child kneels to pray.)

Celebration

Lillian Robbins

Come all of you and gather round
  And hear what I have to say,
This is a special time of year
  When we celebrate Christmas
  Day.

God sent His Son to all of us
  To show us how to live.
We're filled with joy and happiness,
  And gifts we like to give.

We smile and sing and wish you
  well
  And praise God's blessed name.
When we open our hearts and love
  the Lord
  Old things are not the same.

We love each other and want nice
  things,
  But whether we get them or not
In the long run doesn't matter at all.
  Thank God for what we've got.

The Savior who was born in
  Bethlehem
  Came humbly and slept on the
  hay.
His gift to us brings greatest joy
  As we celebrate Christmas Day.

Joyous Greetings

Nell Ford Hann

Boughs of holly, 'round the door,
  Christmas lights aglowing;
Gift-wrapped presents on the floor,
  Outside . . . it's a-snowing!

Christmas JOY fills our hearts,
  With love, peace . . . and living,
'Cause Jesus' birthday's drawing
  nigh,
  The meaning of our giving.

We're going to bake a great big
  cake,
  Decorated with a white dove;
To wish a happy birthday . . . to . . .
  The Jesus that we love.

Perfect, peaceful, holy night,
  Hearts filled with the Spirit,
Love and JOY . . . all that's right,
  So still . . . you can almost hear it.

So friends, family, far and near,
  Our heartfelt wish for you,
The Spirit and meaning of
  Christmas,
  Will last the whole year through.

A Present for Jesus

Orpha A. Thomas

First Child: I'm going to give Jesus a present because it's His birthday.

Second Child: What are you going to give Him?

First Child: I saved a dollar and I'm going to put it in the offering plate at Sunday school.

Second Child: I wish I could give Him some money but I don't have any to give.

First Child: Well, I guess you can't give Him a present this Christmastime.

Second Child *(looking happy)*: Oh, yes I can. I know what I will give Him. I'll just give Him my heart.

Happy Birthday, Jesus

Iris Gray Dowling

(Words to be sung to the tune, "Happy Birthday to You.")

Verse 1:	Happy Birthday, Jesus,
	Happy Birthday, Jesus,
	Baby in a manger stall,
	Born to be Savior of all.
Verse 2:	Jesus is the Savior,
	Jesus is the Savior,
(spell)	S-A-V-I-O-R,
(spell)	S-A-V-I-O-R.
Verse 3:	Jesus loves each of you,
	Jesus loves each of you,
	Jesus died for each of you,
	Jesus loves each of you.

Christmas Kitten

Sharon Kaye Kiesel

One child age 6-8. Need: cat costume or headband cat ears, make-up whiskers/nose, mittens for paws, big bow around neck.

I'm a little Christmas kitten,
Not much bigger than a mitten.
But I've got news to big to keep,
About a love so true and deep.

I've just come from the stable 'round the hill,
Where everything was so dark and still,
I thought I heard a baby cry,
So I went to look, to see who and why.

Into the stable I quietly crept, *(Pretend to creep on tiptoes.)*
And I should have looked before I leapt
For in the manger where the straw was piled,
There was a baby—He saw me—and He smiled!

I know who He is! I truly do!
It's Jesus who's born for me and for you!
Oh glorious gift *(Hug self in excitement.)* from God above—
He's sent us His Son, in eternal love!

~~Good News~~ Christmas Program

Dixie Phillips and Lucy Robbins

"Welcome Christmas Song!" (Tune: "Mary Had a Little Lamb")
(Boy and girl dressed in their Sunday best, carrying helium balloons.)
Girl: We are so glad you came, glad you came, glad you came,
We are so glad you came, to our Christmas play.
Boy: We want to celebrate, celebrate, celebrate,
We want to celebrate, our Lord's birthday.

(A child stands holding a star.)
Child: One little star to show the way.
Where baby Jesus lay.
(Enter three wise men.)
Wise man #1: Let us follow the star to see,
Where the Messiah might be.
Wise man #2: We have three gifts to bring,
To the infant king.
Wise man #3: Wise men still seek Him!
(Enter one angel.)
Angel: An angel came to point the way.
Where the baby Jesus lay.
(Enter two more angels.)
Angel: Peace on earth.
This day of our Lord's birth.
Angel: Good will toward men.
Jesus is born in Bethlehem.
(Enter three shepherds.)
Shepherd #1: Let us leave this flock of sheep.
So we can worship at His feet.
Shepherd #2: What a joy it will be,
To see this holy baby.
Shepherd #3: He will be a king one day.
Let's get started right away.
(Enter Mary, Joseph and baby in a manger.)
Mary: We are humbled that you would come,
To see our little tiny Son.
Joseph: Thank you for all you've done.
This baby is truly God's Son.
(All children stand and face congregation.)

Unison: Won't you come and worship Him, too?

The Shepherds' Surprise

Sharon Kaye Kiesel

Characters: Six children, ages six to eight.
Costumes: Two angels, four shepherds.
Props: Fake fire made from crepe paper with a lighted flashlight under
   it, cutouts of sheep, one or two lamb pillows or lamb toys.

(Sheep and campfire. Shepherds enter carrying lamb.)
Shepherd 1:   Our sheep will be safe here, sheltered by this hill,
Brrr! It's so cold and quiet and still. *(Rubs arms.)*
Let's build up the fire so we'll be warm all night,
For it's many hours till the morning's light.
(Two shepherds tend the fire.)
Shepherd 2: *(Stands, rubs hands together, gazes at sky.)*
The sky is so clear, the stars are so bright!
What's that? *(Points.)* Look—do you see it, that shining light?
What is it? What can it be? It fills the skies,
Listen, do you hear that? This wonder's too great for my eyes!
*(He drops to his knees, hiding his eyes as do the other shepherds. The
angels appear from one side of stage.)*
Angels *(in unison)*:   Fear not! For we bring news of great worth,
The Savior is born! We sing of His birth!
(Shepherds look up but do not stand.)
Angel 1: In the city of David, you'll find Jesus, Lord and King,
Glory to God in the highest! Let your praises ring!
Angel 2: You will find the baby in a manger bed,
Wrapped in cloth, straw cradles His head.
(Angels step back, but not off stage, as shepherds stand.)
Shepherd 3:   Let's go to Bethlehem to see,
That which the Lord has declared to be.
We'll go to the stable so humble and poor,
To see Him—the Savior of the world.
Shepherd 4:   Yes, let us go but a gift we should bring,
To give in worship of Jesus the King.
A lamb would be perfect but only a gift in part—
For to give Jesus the best, we must give Him our hearts.
(Angels and Shepherds sing to the tune of "Away in a Manger.")
The angels first told us of our Savior's birth,
They sang their sweet message high over the earth.
God sent His Son Jesus to save us from sin,
Give glory to God, and peace to all men.

Christmas Candles

Sharon Kaye Kiesel

Cast: Seven children ages nine to eleven.

Costumes: Candles or poster board cutouts to represent candles. The candlelighter carries a cutout of a match.

Candlelighter: These Christmas candles when burning bright,
Shine with a message this holy night.
They are symbols of what our lives should be,
When Jesus shines through you and me.

(Candlelighter touches each "Candle" before that candle recites.)

Blue Candle: My color is the blue of the sky above—
True blue is the color of God's bountiful love.
Blue is the color for Heaven and King,
Of peace and love only Jesus can bring.

White Candle: White is the color of purity and right,
Of forgiveness and love and God's great might.
Jesus, the pure lamb, God, here on earth,
A holy sacrifice from the day of birth.

Green Candle: Green is for faith, for hope, for growing,
For life everlasting, for love ever flowing.
The substance of hope, proof of the unseen,
Eternity's promise in this light of green.

Red Candle: Red is the color of unyielding love,
The gift of the Father from Heaven above.
The gift of the Father, His only Son,
The gift of life that's only begun.

Yellow Candle: The brightest yellow, like a crown of gold,
Promised to believers from centuries old.
Jesus our Redeemer, born to this strife,
A shining star, our crown of life.

Purple Candle: Purple is the color that royalty wears,
Purple for the King born in a manger there,
Jesus who left Heaven and glories behind,
Becoming a true treasure for seekers to find.

Candlelighter: Christmas candles shining bright,
Bringing hope and peace this Christmas night,
Shine forth the love from Jesus who cares,
In the world—He's always there!

Long Ago

Sheila A. Smith

Solo 1: A mule carried two weary travelers to Bethlehem.
Chorus: Long ago.
Solo 2: No room was found in the inn.
Chorus: Long ago.
Solo 3: The Savior was born in a stable of wood and stone.
Chorus: Long ago.
Solo 4: He was wrapped in soft clothes and laid in a manger.
Chorus: Long ago.
Solo 5: Holy was the night.
Chorus: Long ago.
Solo 6: Angelic choirs proclaimed the wondrous story.
Chorus: Long ago.
Solo 7: Shepherds were so afraid.
Chorus: Long ago.
Solo 8: A miraculous star blazed brightly in the dark night.
Chorus: Long ago.
Solo 9: Some wise and wealthy men followed the star.
Chorus: Long ago.
Solo 10: Riches were given to the child.
Chorus: Long ago.
Solo 11: The child grew in wisdom and stature.
Chorus: Long ago.
Solo 12: The child became a man.
Chorus: Long ago.
Solo 13: Many believed He was the promised Messiah.
Chorus: Long ago.
Solo 14: The King was crucified on a cross.
Chorus: Long ago.
Solo 15: He was buried in a borrowed tomb.
Chorus: Long ago.
Solo 16: He arose after three days.
Chorus: Long ago.
Solo 17: He was seen by five hundred people.
Chorus: Long ago.
Solo 18: He ascended into Heaven.
Chorus: Long ago.
Solo 19: These events were recorded in the Bible.
Chorus: Long ago. And today we remember and honor the King of kings and Lord of lords of long ago.

The Christmas Point

Janet Sisk

Processional Song *(congregation and children):* "O Come, All Ye Faithful" *(first two verses)*

Children: *(Some secular Christmas song.)*

Skit *(performed by children)*: "Missing the Point"

Song *(congregation and children):* "Joy to the World" *(four verses)*

Scripture *(read by children):* Luke 2:1-7

Song *(preschool, kindergarten and first grade)*: "Away in a Manger" *(two verses);* "O Little Town of Bethlehem" *(two verses);* "As Each Happy Christmas" *(two verses)*

Scripture *(read by children):* Luke 2:8-20

Song *(second, third and fourth grades):* "While Shepherds Watched Their Flocks"; "We Three Kings of Orient Are"; "The First Noel" *(two verses of each)*

Scripture *(read by children):* Luke 2:21-35

Song *(fifth and sixth grades):* "A Great and Mighty Wonder"; "What Child Is This?" *(three verses of each)*

Scripture *(read by children):* Luke 2:36-40

Song *(congregation and children):* "Angels We Have Heard on High"; "Silent Night! Holy Night!" *(three verses of each).*

Sermonette *(with the theme about the point of Christmas)*

Offering

Prayer

Benediction

Recessional Song *(congregation and children):* "Hark! the Herald Angels Sing" *(two verses)*

Missing the Point

Janet Sisk

This skit can be included in the program outline on the preceding page.

Characters: Mother, Father, Boy, Girl

Scene opens with Mother sitting at a table untangling Christmas lights and decorations. She has a frustrated attitude and facial expression and is mumbling to herself. Boy and Girl are sitting on the floor playing a board game. Props include a card table covered with cloth, two chairs, a Christmas tree and a board game.

Dad *(comes into room looking tired and haggard):* Hi, what's for dinner?
Boy: Hi, Dad!
Girl: Hi, Dad!
Mother: Hello. I'm sorry Dear, I haven't had time to make dinner. I had so much to do today, I just haven't had time to think of cooking. We will have to order out. *(Still frustrated she looks back to the tangled decorations, continues to work with them and says,)* The holiday season just wears me out.
Dad: Okay, where should I go get dinner. I am starved.
Mother: Oh, I don't care. How about pizza? I don't believe it. Two days before Christmas we still have shopping, there are still things to do for the party. I'll never get done. I'm almost to the point I dread the holidays.
Dad *(sits down in the chair to read the newspaper):* I know what you mean. The store has been hectic and every nut and his brother has been in the store in the last month.

Boy *(looking up at his father):* Dad, we haven't been to see Santa yet.

Dad *(without looking away from his paper):* Well you may just have to send him a letter. We may not have time this year.

Mother *(slaps the decorations down on the table in frustration):* I'll never get these untangled.

Dad *(looking up from his paper at mom):* Come on, let's order some food.

Girl: Mommy. *(As she gets up from the floor. She starts approaching her mother, reaching in her pocket and pulling out a piece of paper.)* Mommy will you help me learn my song for the Christmas Eve service.

Mother *(looking at her daughter):* What song?

Girl *(coming to her mother's side):* The one I am going to sing in church.

Mother *(with surprise and some irritation in expression):* When?

Girl: Christmas Eve.

Dad *(looking up from his paper):* Oh Cindy, we can't go to church on Christmas Eve. We'll just have to miss church this year. We're having the family over Christmas Eve and then a Christmas party and dinner on Christmas Day.

Girl: But my Sunday school teacher said we should be there, God likes to hear us sing.

Mother: I am sorry. I'll call and order a pizza. *(Mother, still slightly frustrated but better, starts to get up from the chair.)*

Boy: Oh Cindy, you are silly, nobody cares if you are there or not. *(Boy looks up at girl as he says this.)*

(Mom, just out of the chair and on her way to the phone, stops and looks at her son. Dad looks up from his paper at his son. Both have a surprised look on their faces.)

Boy: They just feed you that baby Jesus birthday stuff to get you to go to church. I like presents, not boring old church.

(Mother and Dad look shocked. They look at each other, back at their son and back at each other.)

Mother: Oh my. John did you hear that?

Dad: We have really done it haven't we?

Mother: We sure have. We have forgotten what Christmas is. We have been worrying about presents, parties, and decorations and forgotten that the birth of our Lord Jesus Christ is the reason for Christmas. And now listen to what we have taught our own children.

Dad *(announces to his family):* The plans for Christmas Eve have changed. Now we will be going to the Christmas Eve church service and we will invite the family to come also. I think it is time we got our priorities straight. You know it is a good thing for us that God doesn't take care of us in the same way we take care of Him. He is more loving and merciful then we are.

18

We Saw Jesus!

Judy Carlsen

Bible-time Christmas Play

This play is designed for easy production. Special lighting is not needed, but a spotlight may be used. Enlarged cutouts of the animals add to the play, as do a life-size manger scene, but they are not necessary. Risers or stairs in the sanctuary or auditorium are useful. This play is helpful for the smaller church that wants each Sunday school student (for example: preschool through sixth grade) to take part in the Christmas program. One or two narrators may be used—perhaps junior high students. Narrators can either use a lectern off to the side or remain behind the scenes with a microphone. The oldest group of students goes on stage first, followed by progressively younger groups, until the very youngest group comes on stage. In this way, the older students remain on stage to sing along with the younger ones. If risers are available, the older students can sit down on the risers while the younger children say their parts.

Scene 1—The Donkey
Scene 2—The Cow
Scene 3—The Sheep
Scene 4—The Camel

Props: Large cutouts of the four animals on heavy cardboard or wood. Large figures of Mary, Joseph and baby Jesus in the manger. (Optional) Large cardboard box (fourth side cut out) to be the stable for the Christmas story.

Introduction

Narrator 1: Can you imagine being on the scene when Jesus was born in Bethlehem? Have you ever thought about it? It must have been exciting to watch firsthand the life-changing events of that special night!

Narrator 2: Luke 2 and Matthew 2 tell us the important parts of the story. It may surprise you to know that most of the animals we often associate with Christmas are not mentioned in the Bible.

Narrator 1: But, it makes sense that animals were there. Stables house farm animals. Shepherds take care of sheep. Most likely, the wise men had camels, since they rode across deserts.

Narrator 2: So, we would like to present to you the Christmas story from the animals' point of view. It's entitled "We Saw Jesus!"

Scene 1

(Fourth—Sixth graders go up on stage. "Donkey" carries picture of donkey and holds until finished speaking, then places next to manger.)

1: Luke 2:1 says the Roman emperor made a decision to count everyone in the empire. So, all the people had to go back to their hometowns to register.

2: Joseph, a carpenter, lived in Nazareth. But, his family was from Bethlehem—at least three days' journey.

3: Joseph didn't like the idea of making this long trip with his wife Mary about to have a baby. But, it had to be done.

Donkey: So, Joseph scraped his pennies together and bought me—a weathered old donkey—for Mary to ride on. It was quite a trip! Mary was heavy! After all, she was about to have her baby!

4: The roads back then were just dirt, with lots of rocks and ruts to make walking difficult. So, it must not have been an easy journey.

Donkey: No, it sure wasn't an easy trip! But, I'm a persistent old donkey. Some call me stubborn. I prefer to say I don't give up easily! Mary and Joseph were kind to me. We stopped for a rest by a stream every few hours or so.

5: Late in the evening of the third day, Mary and Joseph finally arrived—bone tired—in Bethlehem. But, their journey was not over yet!

6: There were people everywhere! Bethlehem was filled with travelers because of the census.

7: Joseph knocked on the door of every inn he could find in Bethlehem. But, every room in every inn was taken! What could he do?

1: Joseph must have been praying to God for help as he wearily knocked at one last inn door. Once again, he heard the same old words, "Sorry, there's no room."

2: The kind man must have seen how tired Joseph was. And maybe he saw the very-pregnant Mary half asleep on the donkey. He took pity on them and said, "I do have a stable out back. It's not much, but at least it is shelter for the night."

Donkey: We wearily trudged into that dark stable. I know I was ready to sleep after such a long journey! Poor Mary just lay down on the straw right next to me and was instantly asleep. Only a short while later, though, I suddenly woke up to the sounds of groaning. I opened my eyes and saw in the dim light of a small lantern that Mary was having her baby!

3: The baby was a healthy boy. Mary and Joseph lovingly wrapped him in strips of cloth to keep him warm.

4: "His name is Jesus," Joseph announced happily.

5: Mary nodded as she joyfully looked at her son. "He is our Lord and Savior."

Donkey: I have to tell you—it was a wonderful sight! Jesus was a special baby. I was happy I could have a small part in helping Mary. Not bad for an old donkey on his last legs, right?

Song: "The Donkey's Song" *(tune: "Mary Had a Little Lamb")*

Long ago a donkey cried,
"I feel old, I'm so old.
What use can I be to God?
For no one here needs me."

God looked down and saw this mule,
Old and gray, feeling down.
God said, "I know what I need,
A donkey who can help."

"Mary needs a steady ride,
One who can carry her
To the town of Bethlehem
Where Jesus will be born."

Now the donkey feels so good,
God used him for His plan.
He can praise the Lord our God
By helping all he can.

Scene 2

Song: "Away in a Manger"—*(a vocal solo or piano solo, perhaps by one of the older students)*
(Third graders come up on stage. Cow 1 carries picture of the cow, then places it next to manger after Cow 5 is finished with his part.)

1: Baby Jesus needed a place to sleep. So, Mary and Joseph used what was there in the stable—the manger.

2: A manger is a wooden open box raised above the ground, so cows can eat their hay.

3: Cows are gentle, kind animals. Have you ever wondered how this cow felt when she saw the baby Jesus lying in her manger?

Cow 1:   Early each morning
And every night
The farmer takes my milk—
Creamy and white.

Cow 2:   I don't mind sharing
What I can give.
That's how God made me.
That's how I live.

Cow 3:   But something's happened
To the place where I munch
My delicious hay—
There's a Boy in my lunch!

Cow 4:   I hear that He's special—
A gift from above.
From God who sent Him
To show folks His love.

Cow 5:   So what can I say?
I just have a hunch
That I have been honored
To have this Boy in my lunch!

Song: "In a Manger Jesus Lay" *(tune: "Jesus Loves Me." Song sung by all children on stage, third—sixth graders.)*

In a manger Jesus lay,
Bedded down among the hay.
Cows looked down at his small form
Asking why this boy was born.

He came to save us *(3 times)*,
To save us from our sins.

Scene 3

Narrator 1: Luke 2 tells us that outside of Bethlehem there were shepherds with their flocks of sheep. All was quiet and still. Everyone was sleeping.

Narrator 2: Suddenly, they were awakened by a bright light! An angel from God appeared, waking the shepherds up in a hurry! They were terrified!

Narrator 1: "Don't be afraid!" the angel said. "I've come to tell you some good news! Today the Savior has been born in Bethlehem. He is Christ the Lord! You'll find him wrapped in cloths and lying in a manger."

Narrator 2: All of a sudden, the sky was filled with angels! They praised God and said, "Glory to God in the highest, and on earth peace, good will to men."

Narrator 1: Then, the angels disappeared! The shepherds must have rubbed their eyes and looked at each other in amazement. "Did we really see and hear all that?" they asked each other.

Song: "O Holy Night!," "While Shepherds Watched Their Flocks" or "Hark! the Herald Angels Sing"—*(vocal or instrumental solo, or perhaps a duet or trio)*

(First and second graders come up on stage. Sheep 1 carries picture, then places it near manger after Sheep 6 is finished.)

Sheep 1:   The angels said to go
To Bethlehem tonight,
So we the sheep will go
And follow the star's light.

Sheep 2:   We go with all our flock
To see this special Boy.
He's Jesus, God's own Son.
Our hearts are filled with joy!

Sheep 3:   When we came to the barn
Where baby Jesus lay,
We bowed and worshiped Him—
Our Savior in the hay.

Sheep 4:   Then we went out and told
The people everything:
That Jesus Christ was born
To someday be our King.

Sheep 5:   Oh, may you be like sheep
Who saw the infant King,
And go and tell the news
That Jesus came to bring.

Sheep 6:   Good news we have to tell
About this Boy so small.
He is the Lamb of God
And Savior of us all.

Scene 4

Narrator 1: After Jesus was born in Bethlehem, the gospel writer Matthew tells us in chapter 2 that wise men came from the East, looking for the king of the Jews.

Narrator 2: They said they had followed the king's star. Naturally, they went first to Jerusalem, the capital city, in their search for this new king.

Narrator 1: King Herod was first surprised and then angry when he heard this news. He called in the priests who knew the Scriptures and asked where this king, the Messiah, was supposed to be born. They found the answer in Micah 5:2—He was to be born in Bethlehem.

Narrator 2: Herod told the wise men to find the new king and then report back to him, so he could go and worship him too. So, the wise men continued their journey. They were overjoyed that the special star was again leading them.

Narrator 1: By this time, Mary and Joseph were living in a house in Bethlehem. Jesus was at least a few months old. When the wise men came to the house, they bowed down before this little king and worshiped Him.

Narrator 2: They gave Him valuable gifts—gold, frankincense and myrrh. Their long search was ended!

Narrator 1: God told them in a dream to go back home another way and not tell Herod where Jesus was. So, they went home, rejoicing to be a part of those welcoming the new King.

(Preschoolers and Kindergarteners come up on stage. One brings the picture of the camel and places it by the manger. The following four lines can be handled one of two ways: either as parts for four children, or as a unison four-line part for all the small children.)

1. We are the camels the wise men rode, *(Pretend to ride.)*
2. Over the hills, through hot and cold. *(Show hills, then fan, then shiver.)*
3. We carried gifts to give to the boy, *(Give gifts.)*
4. Then left to go home, full of great joy. *(Smile and ride.)*

(All children sing together the rest of the songs.)

Song: "Jesus Was a Baby Born in Bethlehem" *(Tune: "The Joy of the Lord")*

1. Oh, Jesus was a baby born in Bethlehem. (3 times)
   We love Him and we praise His holy name.
2. Oh, Jesus came to earth to set the people free. (3 times)
   We love Him and we praise His holy name.
3. We worship and we praise Him on this Christmas Day. (3 times)
   We love Him and we praise His holy name.

Songs: "Clap Your Hands" (by Jimmy and Carol Owens)
"Rejoice in the Lord Always"

Narrator 1: These animals were excited to see Jesus! The donkey
carried Mary to Bethlehem. The cow loaned her manger to Jesus for
His first bed.

Narrator 2: The sheep were the first visitors to see the newborn King.
They spread the good news to everyone they saw! Then, the camels
came, bringing priceless gifts to honor the young Savior.

Narrator 1: Even though we are not animals, we can be servants to our
Savior just as they were. Like the donkey, we can be hard-working—
never giving up. Like the cow, we can share what we have to help
others. Jesus said that when we help others, we are really helping Him.

Narrator 2: Like the sheep, we can joyfully tell the good news of the
Gospel to everyone we meet. And like the camels, we can give Jesus
the very best we are and have.

Narrator 1: As you celebrate Christmas this year, remember the animals
of the Christmas story. And rejoice! For, Jesus reigns!

Song: "Jesus, Name Above All Names"
(Audience joins in second time.)

Do You Hear What I Hear?

Agnes Chabot

This is a very simple program. It would lend itself well to a "center stage" version in a school or church hall without a stage. The children could sit on three sides, facing the stage, with the audience behind them. On cue, each group could go to their places in the tableau. Speaking groups could stand and face the audience to say their pieces. In this setting, the kings could be seated with their class, get up, and wander through the audience before joining the nativity scene.

When we produced this program, our main objective was to give each primary child a costume or a speaking part. The grade one and two girls were angels. The boys from grade two were shepherds and the grade one boys were, of course, the sheep. The grade threes were kings, servants, speakers, and the welcome readers. Kindergarteners were the children in costumes from other lands and looked adorable. The grade sevens did the readings, made props and sang the carol for the angels. The grade sixes sang the main carol. The fours and fives each had one special carol and sang the other one together.

(Choir enters while music plays softly.)

Carol: "Do You Hear What I Hear?" *(entire carol, Grade 6)*
Welcome *(read by three or four children together):* Welcome to our
  program. We would like to share the Christmas story with you.
(Curtain opens on the manger scene. Hills and grass can be seen at one side of the stage.)
Carol: "Do You Hear What I Hear?" *(verse one—Grade 6)*
(Child hangs star above the stable.)
Reading: Luke 2:1-5
(Mary and Joseph walk across the stage and then go to manger and sit down. Baby is already in manger.)
Reading: Luke 2:6, 7
Carol: "O Bambino" *(Grade 5)*
Carol: "Do You Hear What I Hear?" *(verse two—Grade 6)*
(Shepherds and sheep take places on grass. Shepherds huddle around fire.)
Reading: Luke 2: 8, 9
(Angels appear on stage.)

Angels: Be not afraid. We bring you tidings of great joy. For unto you is born this very night in Bethlehem a Savior. You will find the babe wrapped in swaddling clothes and lying in a manger.

Carol: "Angels We Have Heard on High" *(Grade 7)*
(Angels, shepherds and sheep move to the manger to form tableau.)
Carol: "Do You Hear What I Hear?" *(verse three—Grade 6)*
Reading: Matthew 2:1, 2 and 9-11
Carol: "We Three Kings" *(Grades 4 and 5)*
(Wise men enter from the back. They proceed down center aisle, stopping on chorus to gaze at star. Each king presents his gift while choir sings appropriate verse, then joins the tableau.)
Carol: "Do You Hear What I Hear?" *(verse four—Grade 6)*
(Then sing entire carol through.)
(Kindergarten children in costumes from other nations enter and present gifts. They take their places at the side of the stage.)
Carols: "Away in a Manger" and "Let There Be Peace." *(sung by entire cast)*
Announcer *(asks audience to join in carols, announce each in turn)*:
"The First Noel," "Silent Night," "O Come, All Ye Faithful"
Announcer: Thank you for being with us this evening. We hope you have enjoyed our program. We would like to wish you a merry Christmas.
Carol: "We Wish You a Merry Christmas"—*(all children)*

The Birthing

Dorothy M. Page

Characters:
Aven, the Innkeeper
Rachah, Innkeeper's wife
Mary
Joseph
Shepherds #1, #2 and #3
Angel Chorus

Time: Time of the birth of Jesus

Costumes: Biblical costumes of usual type used in program for
 Christmas. Mary in pale blue with white veil. Joseph in navy or brown
 robe. Angels in filmy white robes with gilt or silver trim.

Scene 1: An outdoor scene, a few trees, rocks, etc. Any item to give the
 impression of the grounds of the inn where Jesus was born.
Scene 2: Same as Scene 1.
Scene 3: The manger.

Props: potted trees, palms, etc. (real or artificial); a few rocks; a plain
 bench. The usual props for a manger scene.

SCENE 1

The setting as suggested. Innkeeper's wife walks onstage.

Shepherd #1 *(runs on after her)*: Where are my brother shepherds?
Rachah: I have seen no shepherds.
Shepherd #1: I was separated from them in the crowd of visitors to
 Bethlehem. We have come to see the Christ child.
Rachah: The Christ child?
Shepherd #1: Yes. While we were in the field caring for our flocks, a
 great light shone in the sky and an angel came down from the light.
 The angel told us not to be afraid because he was bringing us good
 news. He said that a baby born in a manger in Bethlehem was the
 Christ child, the promised Messiah.

Rachah: Why have you come to this place?

Shepherd #1: The angel told us we would find the baby wrapped in swaddling clothes and lying in a manger. Your inn has a stable doesn't it?

Rachah: Yes, we do.

Shepherd #1: Is there a baby in the stable?

Rachah: Yes. A baby boy was born to the couple who stayed in our stable last night. I knew there was something unusual about those people. I begged my husband to make room for them in the inn.

Shepherd #1: I am going to the stable to see the child.

Curtain

(During this brief pause music such as one of the favorite Christmas carols "O Little Town of Bethlehem," or "While Shepherds Watched Their Flocks," etc. can be used to enhance the program.)

SCENE 2

Same scene. Innkeeper and Rachah come onstage. She is carrying a blanket.

Aven *(shouting):* I am weary of hearing you babble of a Christ child.

Rachah: Aven, I begged you to make room for them in the inn. I wanted to give them our bed, but you said they would probably not be able to pay the price: the unfair price you are charging those who come to Bethlehem for the census. Putting that couple in the stable was a mistake. We will be punished for that.

Aven *(angrily):* Punished! I have done nothing wrong. Why should I be punished?

Rachah: I have been troubled about this. If this is the Christ child we will be punished for sending them to the stable.

Aven: Superstitious woman! The Christ child? Bah! How can you believe such nonsense? They are just poor travelers. The woman should not have come on so long a journey. Is it my fault she chose to be foolish? I will hear no more of this.

Rachah: But the angels. One of the shepherds said that an angel told them they would find the baby wrapped in swaddling clothes, lying in a manger in Bethlehem.

Aven: And you believe such nonsense?

Rachah: Well, I'm taking this warm blanket for the baby.

Aven: We have need of such for our paying guests. You will not take that blanket to the stable. *(He moves toward her.)*

Rachah *(draws back)*: Remember the angels said the Christ child was born in Bethlehem. I believe this is the Christ child. *(She hurries offstage.)*

(Aven shrugs, shakes his head, then throws up his arms and walks offstage muttering.)

Curtain

SCENE 3

Manger scene. Two shepherds kneeling, Shepherd #1 is standing in background. Mary and Joseph and manger in foreground.)

Rachah *(enters, speaks to Mary)*: I am Rachah, wife of Aven, the innkeeper. I regret that we had no room for you in the inn. May I wrap the little one in this warm blanket?

Mary: A warm blanket will be welcome.

Rachah *(tenderly wraps the baby in the blanket)*: There little one, now you will be warm.

Joseph: We are grateful to you for your kindness.

Rachah *(stares at the baby)*: Is this baby truly the promised Christ child? *(Rachah looks very frightened. Just then Aven enters and stands watching.)*

Mary: This child is truly the Christ child. You must not be afraid.

Aven *(goes to Rachah and kneels by her)*: I am truly sorry Rachah for my angry words. I believe this is the Christ child. Let us worship Him together.

(A group of angels come onstage and sing "Joy to the World.")

NOTE: The program could end with the audience joining with the angel chorus.

Christmas Around the World

Kathryn Christensen

This play is designed for children from three-year-olds through grade school, but can use the older children as narrators. There are enough parts that an entire Sunday school program could participate. It is easy to produce as there are few props. Many of the props can be made by the children in their Sunday school classes. The stage design stays the same through the first seven acts with a simple change for the last act.

This skit is divided into eight acts distinguished by the change in country. Each act can accommodate an unlimited number of children, but needs a minimum of six. In addition to these children, an unlimited number of angels are needed. Also required is a narrator, or the part can be divided among several narrators. Narrators can be a teacher or older children. A piano player adds a nice touch.

Scriptures quoted from the *International Children's Bible, New Century Version,* copyright ©1986, 1988 by Word Publishing, Dallas, Texas 75039. Used by permission.

Act 1: United States
Act 2: France
Act 3: Mexico
Act 4: Germany

Act 5: England
Act 6: Korea
Act 7: Sweden
Act 8: Holy Land

Stage Design: Acts 1-7: The stage is the same in the first seven parts. An undecorated Christmas tree is needed. It should be placed to one side of the stage. A fireplace made from a sturdy furniture box should be placed in the center of the stage toward the back. A small table can be put in a visible, but non-intrusive place. **Act 8**: Remove fireplace and small table. Place stable, made from appliance box, center stage. Add a manger (a small box or doll cradle) with straw or crumpled newspaper and blanket. Hang star from ceiling or attach to top of stable.

Costumes: Most of the children can wear what they would like. There are a few parts that require a costume and that information is listed below.

Angels: White robe-like outfit, may have wings attached to back. May use halo made from paper or tinsel garland.

Kristkind (Germany): Long white dress with red sash. Crown made from a tinsel garland and pipe cleaners for candles.

Hans Trapp (Germany): He should wear a pair of lederhosens, if available. Otherwise shorts and a white shirt will do.

Korean Children (Korea): If available the hanbok dress should be worn.

Lucia (Sweden): Long white dress with red sash. A garland crown can be made from tinsel garland.

Mary (Holy Land): White robe-like outfit.

Angel (Holy Land): White robe-like outfit with halo made from paper or tinsel garland. May attach wings made from cardboard and construction paper or fabric.

Joseph, Shepherds and Wise Men (Holy Land): Bathrobes or other draped-robe style clothing.

Props: The props for each act will be described as they are introduced.

Procedure: If you have a piano player, have her play a medley of Christmas carols as the audience enters and is seated. The narrator begins the program by reading the first part. Have the piano player play a chosen Christmas song softly in the background during the opening oration. Stage directions will be given with each act.

Script

Narrator: Christmas is one of the most celebrated holidays of Christians around the world. It is a time set aside to celebrate the birth of Jesus Christ nearly 2,000 years ago. An important part of the Christmas celebration is worship. All over the world people come together on Christmas Eve in love and friendship to rejoice in the birth of the Holy Child. Christians universally worship with music, drama, symbols, candles and gift-giving to express their faith with love, joy and hope.

Also part of the Christmas celebrations are carols, cantatas, pageants of the Christmas story, candlelight services and gifts to the needy. Christmas cards and hymns have been written in almost every language.

Almost every country has its own Christmas customs. Many of these customs, celebrations and legends have pagan beginnings. For example, when the pagans of northern Europe became Christians they made their sacred evergreen trees a part of the Christian festival and decorated them with gilded nuts and candles to represent the stars, moon and sun.

Gift giving has always been part of the Christmas revelry. The gift giver in early times was someone shadowy and mysterious, whose home was in some remote place like Heaven or the North Pole. He visited children on horseback or on a sleigh drawn by reindeer. Some of these bearers of gifts were St. Nicholas, the Three Kings, and Knight Rupprecht. In central and northern Europe St. Nicholas arrived with the Archangel Gabriel. The Angel Gabriel was also reported to be responsible for a miracle in France. A rose is said to have bloomed when the Angel touched the ground with his staff, so the little girl who accompanied the shepherds would have flowers to give the baby Jesus.

Of course, angels played a most important part in the Christmas story. They brought the good news to Mary and Joseph that she would give birth to the son of God. The angels also appeared to the shepherds proclaiming the nativity.

Speaking of angels, here they are now.

(Piano player plays "Hark! the Herald Angels Sing" while the angels enter with banners of United States and walk through audience. Adult should accompany them. This routine is repeated after each country is represented.)

Props: The banners should be the flag of the country. Make flags from construction paper and staple them to dowels purchased at a building supply store. Flag patterns can be found in the encyclopedia. Tie jingle bells on gold ribbon about three feet apart. Have each angel carry one bell. This helps keep all the little angels together!

Act 1: United States

Narrator: The American Christmas is a patchwork of traditions from around the world. Many of our traditions come from England and Germany. For example, Americans have made the German tree decorating an important part of their holiday.
(Have two or more children place a typically American decoration on the Christmas tree. Have them stand to side of stage.)

Another important tradition is hanging stockings. On Christmas Eve, American children hang stockings over the fireplace or at the ends of their beds. Sometimes they write letters to Santa to tell him what they want for Christmas.

(Have two or more children hang stockings on the fireplace. Have them join the other children at side of stage.)

Many American homes are decorated with holly at Christmas. This tradition comes from an old fable. When the shepherds rushed to the stable to see baby Jesus, they did not see the tiny lamb that followed after the shepherd boy who had been caring for him. This little lamb was weak and ill and its bleating was too faint to be heard when it stumbled on the rough ground and scratched itself on the prickly holly bushes.

When Mary saw the boy picking up the lamb to comfort it, and warm it in his cloak, she said, "My son will be kind to smaller creatures, just as you are. Your kindness to the little lamb will always be remembered." So now we use the holly with the red winter berries to remind us of the lamb and the kind boy.

(Have two or more children enter with holly and put it on the fireplace or under the tree.)

All Children Perform:

Poem: Holly berries shining bright
Remind us of that great night
When Jesus came to us with love
From our heavenly Father above.

Bible Verse: "The angel said to her, 'Don't be afraid, Mary, because God is pleased with you . . . . You will give birth to a son, and you will name him Jesus'" (Luke 1:30, 31).

Song: "Greensleeves"—one verse

Props: 1. Christmas tree decorations that are traditionally American.
2. Christmas stockings (real or made from construction paper).
3. Holly branches or a holly wreath. If not available in someone's yard, they can be purchased at a garden store.

Act 2: France

Narrator: Here come the angels again flying off to France to herald the good news.

(Enter angels and adult with banners of France. Walk through audience.)

Narrator: Christmas trees in France are decorated with many different colored stars. On Christmas Eve toys, candies and fruits are added to the tree.

(Two or more children place colored stars on tree. Toys or candy or fruit could also be used. Have them stand to side of stage.)

Narrator: Instead of stockings hanging on the fireplace, French children place their shoes in front of the fire where Pere Noel, Father Christmas, fills them on Christmas Eve. Birch sticks are sometimes left as a reminder to be good.

(Two or more children place shoes by fireplace.)

Narrator: Creche, the French word for cradle, has come to mean any manger scene. Monks in the Thirteenth Century introduced it to remind people of the true meaning of Christmas. Churches in France often have a living creche with real people and animals. Children are invited to come to the manger to sing lullabies to the baby Jesus.

(Two or more children place a manger scene on the little table. If old enough, have them sing a short lullaby.)

All Children Perform:

Poem: Stars on trees bring bright light.
               All over France on Christmas night
               Shoes are placed near the fire with joy
               So Santa can fill them with lots of toys.

Bible Verse: "While Joseph and Mary were in Bethlehem, the time came for her to have the baby. She gave birth to her first son. There were no rooms left in the inn. So she wrapped the baby with cloths and laid him in a box where animals are fed" (Luke 2:6, 7).

Song: French Christmas Carol, "The Friendly Beasts"

Props: 1. Stars made from different colored construction paper and decorated with glitter. Use ribbon as hangers.
2. Children's shoes.
3. Small manger scene.

Act 3: Mexico

Narrator: Leaving Europe the angels head south to Mexico.
(Angels enter with adult carrying Mexican flags. Walk through audience.)
Narrator: Mexican Christmas trees are decorated with colored-paper lanterns.
(Two or more children put lanterns on tree. Move to side of stage.)
Narrator: As for many Spanish holidays, children enjoy using a pinata on Christmas Eve. This papier-mache container filled with candy and toys hangs by a cord from a tree or any place else where it can swing freely. The children are blindfolded and try to break it with a stick. When it breaks they scramble for the goodies.
(Two or more children break candy-filled pinata.)
Narrator: The weather is warm this time of year in Mexico so flowers can be used for decorations. There is an old Mexican tale of a little girl who was so poor she had no money to buy a present to take to the manger at the church. As she stood sadly outside watching others carrying in presents, she began to clear away the tall weeds hiding the stone angel in front of the chapel. Suddenly, she heard a voice saying, "Take these weeds into the church and the Christ child will bless them and you."

With an armful of weeds, she went into the church and up to the manger. As she walked the tops of the weeds turned bright red, as if they had burst into flames. Since then these flowers, named poinsettias, have been used at Christmas in many parts of the world.
(Children bring poinsettias and place on fireplace or near tree).

All Children Perform:

Poem: A pinata filled with candy and toys
            Is a Mexican game for girls and boys.
            In Mexico the poinsettias bloom
            To colorfully fill a Christmas room.

Bible Verse: "That night, some shepherds were in the fields nearby watching their sheep. An angel of the Lord stood before them. The glory of the Lord was shining around them, and suddenly they became very frightened. The angel said to them, 'Don't be afraid, because I am bringing you some good news. It will be a joy to all the people. Today your Savior was born in David's town. He is Christ, the Lord" (Luke 2:8-11).

Song: Mexican Christmas Carol, "Fum, Fum, Fum"

(Teacher's tip: this is a fairly difficult song to learn. If you have younger children you might want to substitute it with an easier carol.)

Props: 1. Make paper lanterns from construction paper.
2. Pinatas can be purchased at party shops or import shops for very little money. They can also be made from papier-mache. Sticks for breaking pinata. Candy for inside.
3. Poinsettias.

Act 4: Germany

Narrator: Back across the ocean, the angels arrive in Germany.
(Angels enter, with adult, carrying banners of Germany.)
Narrator: Seeing their tree for the first time Christmas Eve, is one of the most exciting moments of the holiday for German children. It is decorated secretly by the mother with stars, angels, tiny toys, gingerbread, nuts and candy.

One beloved German fable tells of a woodman's family on Christmas Eve. As they sat snugly around the fire, there was a knock at the door. Much to their surprise a small boy was standing outside in the snowy forest, all alone. They invited him in and gave him warm food and drink and bed for the night.

The next morning they were awakened by the singing of a choir of angels, whose presence filled the cottage with light. The woodman's family realized they had given shelter to the Christ child.

"You cared for me," said Jesus, "This will remind me of your visit." As he touched a little fir tree near the door he said, "May this tree glow to warm your hearts. And may it carry presents, so that you are as kind to one another as you are to me."

Another traditional story tells how after a widow had decorated the tree for her children, spiders spun webs all over it. The Christ child, passing by, turned the webs to silver, to delight them on Christmas morning. That is why we put tinsel on our trees.
(Two or more children hang gingerbread men, paper angels, and tinsel on the tree. Have children go to side of stage.)
Narrator: In some parts of Germany, children receive gifts from a girl called Kristkind. She wears a crown of candles and carries a basket of gifts. A terrible demon called Hans Trapp goes with Kristkind and threatens the children who have been naughty with a stick.
(Kristkind and Hans Trapp (see costumes on page 32) come with basket of gifts and sticks. Have Hans Trapp shake stick at Kristkind and the other children on stage.)

Narrator: Advent calendars herald the beginning of the Christmas season for German children. Advent means "coming" and this is the time the Germans prepare for the birth of Christ. The advent calendar has 24 numbered doors to open, one for each day until Christmas Eve. Inside each door is a picture or piece of candy.

Some advent calendars are wreaths of fir branches on which 24 little boxes hang. Each box is wrapped in brightly-colored paper with a number on the outside and present on the inside. One box is opened each day of advent.

(Two or more children come holding advent wreath and calendar and place them on top of fireplace. Have all children line up in the center of the stage.)

All Children Perform:

Poem: We decorate our trees with stars
        With angels, tops and tiny cars.
        Candy, nuts and gingerbread
        On branches hang with golden thread.

Bible Verse: "Then a very large group of angels from heaven joined the first angel. All the angels were praising God, saying:
        'Give glory to God in heaven, and on earth let there be peace to the people who please God.'
Then the angels left the shepherds and went back to heaven. The shepherds said to each other, 'Let us go to Bethlehem and see this thing that has happened. We will see this thing the Lord told us about'" (Luke 2:13-15).

Song: German Christmas Carol, "O Tannenbaum"

Props: 1. Gingerbread men made from brown construction paper and decorated with sequins and rickrack, paper angels and tinsel.
2. See page 32 for Kristkind's costume. Wrap tiny boxes and place them in a basket for her to carry. Hans Trapp's costume is on page 32. He should have a short stick (lummi sticks work well here).
3. Make an advent wreath from a plastic foam hoop covered with green crepe paper. Cut green holly leaves and red berries from construction paper and glue them to the wreath. Hang 24 little presents from the wreath. Have one child hold the wreath and one open one of the presents.

Act 5: England

Narrator: It's off to merry old England where the angels will bring the glad tidings.

(Angels enter, with adult, carrying English flag banners.)

Narrator: The English like to "borrow the tree" for Christmas. They uproot a fir tree from the garden and plant it in a tub. After Christmas they replant it outdoors. Christmas trees in England are topped with the British Crown. Other decorations often include candy sugarplums tucked into ribbon and flower decorated cornucopias or silver filigreed doily baskets.

(Two or more children decorate tree with British Crown and doily baskets. Children go to side of stage.)

Narrator: England was the first country to use Christmas cards. The custom is over 100 years old.

(Enter two or more children carrying Christmas cards. Have them place them on the fireplace. Children go to side of stage.)

Narrator: Other traditions originating in England include fruitcake, plum pudding, mincemeat pie, mistletoe, bells, and, of course, the yule log. The mistletoe plant with its white berries has long been a symbol of friendship in England. In the olden days, if friends met under the mistletoe, it was thought to bring them good luck. If enemies found themselves together under the mistletoe they had to stop fighting. Now, when someone stands under mistletoe they can expect to be kissed.

(Have one child enter and place yule log in fireplace. Have another child bring fruitcake and place it on top of the fireplace. Other children can carry mistletoe. All children go to center of stage.)

All Children Perform:

Poem: England celebrates with glee
With crowns atop the Christmas tree.
A yule log in the fire ablaze
Marks the start of Christmas days.

Bible Verse: "So the shepherds went quickly and found Mary and Joseph. And the shepherds saw the baby lying in a feeding box. Then they told what the angels had said about this child. Everyone was amazed when they heard what the shepherds said to them. Mary hid these things in her heart; she continued to think about them" (Luke 2:16-19).

Song: English Christmas Carol, "Christmas Is Coming"

Props: 1. Make a British Crown from yellow construction paper. Make
   filigreed doily baskets from silver doilies with pipe cleaner handles.
2. Christmas cards.
3. Fireplace wood, mistletoe, holly, fruitcake.

Act 6: Korea

Narrator: The angels take flight again—all the way to Korea.
*(Enter angels, and adult, carrying Korean flags. Walk through the
audience.)*
Narrator: Koreans celebrate Christmas much like Americans only not
   with as much Yankee-Doodle enthusiasm. Their celebration is much
   smaller. Christmas Eve there is a big dinner followed by game playing.
   These games last all night long.
*(Two or more children enter with paddle-ball game and play game. Move
to side of stage.)*
Narrator: The joy of Christmas in Korea is expressed in singing and gift
   giving. One tradition among children is presenting a (joy) gift at the
   church pageant. These gifts are given to orphanages and needy
   families.
*(Have children enter with gifts to place under the tree. Have them join the
other children at the side of stage.)*
Narrator: On Christmas Eve, the Korean Christians parade in the streets
   in large groups carrying paper lanterns lighted with candles and
   decorated with red crosses, singing Christmas carols as they march.
   They meet at 10:30 P.M. in the churches for a two hour service.
   Following the ceremony a special meal of duck kook, or soup with
   duck, Kimchi, rice cakes, fruit and ginger candy is served.
*(Have two or more children enter with paper lanterns decorated with red
crosses and parade across the stage.)*

All Children Perform:

Poem: Christmas Eve the Koreans play,
        Gifts are opened the next day.
        Korean Christians all parade
        Carrying lanterns that they made.

Bible Verse: "The wise men heard the king and then left. They saw the same star they had seen in the east. It went before them until it stopped above the place where the child was. When the wise men saw the star, they were filled with joy" (Matthew 2:9, 10).

Song: "Hark! the Herald Angels Sing"

Props: 1. Paddle ball games.
2. Gifts
3. Lanterns made from construction paper and decorated with red crosses.

Act 7: Sweden

Narrator: We now see the angels leave Korea for the long flight to Sweden.
(Angels and adult enter carrying Swedish flags and walk through audience.)
Narrator: Even before Jesus was born, straw seemed to have magical properties. It was used by farmers to spread over their crops to make them grow better. Since the baby Jesus was probably placed in a straw manger, straw was used by people to make decorations for the tree. Swedish children make goats of straw to guard the tree and keep away the evil spirits. Other Christmas tree decorations are bird nests, little heart-shaped baskets filled with candy and miniature flags of blue and yellow, the national colors of Sweden.
(Two or more children enter and decorate tree with Swedish flags and bird nests. Line up at end of stage.)
Narrator: December 13 is a special day in Sweden. This is the feast of St. Lucia, whose goodness is remembered each year all over Sweden.

Lucia was an early follower of Jesus. In those days, Christians were often treated cruelly. They would hide in underground caves to pray to Jesus. Lucia took them food secretly, in the night, so they wouldn't starve. On her head she wore a crown of candles to light the way as her hands were busy carrying food and drink.

Many Swedish children cook the special Lucia buns and ginger snaps on December 12. The next morning all the children get up early and the youngest girl dresses up as St. Lucia in a long white dress with a red sash. She wears a crown of evergreen with candles to light her way. In her hand is a tray of food for her family.
(Enter the Lucia girl carrying a tray of rolls.)

Her brothers act as Star Boys. They wear special pointed hats covered with stars. At night they go caroling.

(Two or more boys come out with star hats and song books and sing a short Christmas carol.)

All Children Perform:

Poem: In Sweden there is candle making,
Cookie and candy baking.
Star boys go out a'singing
While Christmas bells are ringing.

Bible Verse: "They went to the house where the child was and saw him with his mother, Mary. They bowed down and worshiped the child. They opened the gifts they brought for him. They gave him treasures of gold, frankincense, and myrrh" (Matthew 2:11).

Song: Swedish Christmas Carol, "Christmas Day"

Props: 1. One bird nest, either real, or made from straw. Miniature flags of Sweden made from construction paper.
2. See costume for Lucia girl on page 32. She should carry a tray with rolls.
3. Star hats made from dark blue construction paper. Take paper and form into cone. Stick gold stars around cone and hang a tinsel garland tassel to top of hat. Song books.

Act 8: Holy Land

(Change scenery by removing fireplace and small table. Place stable in the center of the stage and the manger inside. Have piano player play "Away in a Manger" quietly during narration.)

Narrator: The angels last stop is the Holy Land.
(Angels and adult enter carrying flags of Holy Land. Go through audience.)
Narrator: About 2,000 years ago, God sent to earth a Savior for mankind who would be called Jesus. God chose a woman named Mary as the mother of this boy. One day while Mary was at home, an angel appeared to her and told Mary that God had chosen her to be the mother of the blessed Savior of all mankind.

As days and months passed quickly, Joseph and his wife, Mary, prepared and waited patiently for the birth of baby Jesus.

One day Joseph heard that all people had to pay a tax and they could not refuse. *(Send Mary and Joseph onstage.)* So Joseph placed Mary on the back of a donkey and rode from sunrise till sundown until they reached Bethlehem. Because there were so many people there to pay taxes, all of the inns were full. Mary was tired and knew her baby would soon be born. Finally they found an inn whose owner led them to a stable where they could spend the night. Later that evening baby Jesus was born and Mary put him in the manger prepared by her husband, Joseph. *(Have Mary place baby in manger.)*

At that same time, outside the town some shepherds were watching their sheep. *(Have shepherd come out and stand to right of stage. Angel enters also.)* An angel came to them and said, "I bring good tidings of great joy! Our Savior, Christ the Lord is born." Then a heavenly host filled the sky, saying, "Glory to God in the highest! Peace on earth!"

(Wise men enter.) Wise men knowing of the birth had traveled very far. A brightly shining star guided them to the place where Jesus was.

These people gathered round to honor Jesus Christ the Lord. Then each presented Jesus with a priceless gift of love in humble thankfulness for the best gift from God above.

(All children come to center stage and sing "Away in a Manger.")

Props: Stuffed lambs, lantern and staff for Joseph, doll, staff for shepherds, gifts from wise men, *(box wrapped in gold paper; tall wooden pepper mill; ceramic bottle in dark brown),* stable made from large box, box with straw for baby Jesus, large star made of cardboard covered with aluminum foil. For costumes see page 32.

Bibliography

Holy Bible, International Children's Bible, Word Publishing, 1988.

Hole, Christina, *Christmas and Its Customs,* M. Barrows & Co., Inc. 1958.

Hottes, Alfreds Carl, *1001 Christmas Facts and Fancies.* A. T. DeLaMare Co., 1937.

Sechrist, Elizabeth Hough, *Christmas Everywhere!* Roland Swain, Published 1931.

Wernecke, Herbert H., *Celebrating Christmas Around the World,* Westminster Press, 1982.

Wernecke, Herbert H., *Christmas Customs Around the World,* Westminster Press, 1959.

Willson, Robina Beckles, *Merry Christmas—Children at Christmas Time Around the World,* Philomel Books, 1983.

Mr. Grump

Dixie Phillips

This play/cantata is for young people who love to sing. The performers should dress in white shirts or blouses and dark dress pants or skirts. You could go more formal and have them in choir robes. It's up to each individual church to decide.

Characters
Mr. Grump
Selfish Child
Airhead Anne
Jumping Jordan
J. J.'s Dad
Mr. Brown, minister
Readers
Choir

Our play begins with an old man, Mr. Grump, pacing back and forth. He is hunched over with a cane and has a grumpy look on his face.

Mr. Grump: Christmas, Bah . . . Humbug !!!!!!!!!!! Who needs it? What is the true meaning of Christmas anyway?
(Scene changes to other side of platform. A child is looking at a "Wish Book" catalog. She is writing down her Christmas list.)
Selfish Child: Mother, I've just finished my Christmas list. *(She flips out looooooooong calculator paper that will roll down the aisle.)* Oh, I think I forgot something. *(She jots down another item.)*
(Child takes center stage.)
Selfish Child: What do I want for Christmas?
Well, I'll tell you . . .
I've been dreaming about it for weeks.
I want lots and lots of presents
Candy, toys and special little treats.

I've got to have what Jan is getting up the hill.
Oh, and I can't be outdone by my friend, Jill.
If your cash is running low,
Your credit card's the way to go.
That's all . . . all I want for Christmas!

(Scene returns to Mr. Grump.)

Mr. Grump: Christmas, Bah . . . Humbug!!!!! Who needs it? What is the true meaning of Christmas?

(Scene changes to other side of platform to Jumping Jordan and his father.)

Jumping Jordan: But Daddy . . . I just have to have a pair of those new pump tennis shoes. All the other boys on the team have a pair. I'll be the ONLY one that doesn't have a pair. Besides Daddy . . . I heard they really give good ankle support. You wouldn't want your boy to have weak ankles now would you????

J.J.'s Dad: Son, I am NOT paying $100.00 for a pair of tennis shoes.

Jumping Jordan: Awwwww Daddy . . . I hate being poor!

(Scene changes to Mr. Grump.)

Mr. Grump: Christmas, Bah . . . Humbug!!!! Who needs it? What is the true meaning of Christmas?

(Scene changes to Airhead Anne who is talking on the phone.)

Airhead Anne: Hi Tiff, this is little ole ME. I just have to tell you what Eric is giving MEEEEE for Christmas. A diamond ring!!!!! What's that? We're only 15—Oh, I know that Tiff but we are 15 going on 30—we're sooo mature. And my mother is giving me those designer jeans. You know the kind that EVERYBODY who is ANYBODY wears. And listen to this Tiff, Daddy says I can have that new red Porsche. I just LOVE Christmas. It's truly the season of getting *(Clears throat.)* I mean giving. It's too bad that your daddy lost his job. Maybe you'd be getting a pair of those jeans too. See ya at school! Bye!

(Scene returns to Mr. Grump.)

Mr. Grump: Christmas, Bah . . . Humbug!!! Who needs it? People are only out to make money. They don't really care about anyone.

Mr. Grump: I'm a grumpy old man you see.
        And nobody really loves me.
        I don't have a friend,
        On whom I can depend,
        Cause I'm just plain old grumpy!!!

(A knock at the door is heard.)

Mr. Grump: Go away!

Mr. Brown: Samuel . . . Samuel Jacobs . . . It's me, Mr. Brown. May I come in?

Mr. Grump: Oh, I suppose if you have to.

Mr. Brown: Samuel, it's good to see you. I wanted to invite you to our Christmas program tonight.

Mr. Grump: Why? Are you going to take up an offering?

Mr. Brown: Well, no Samuel we aren't planning to!

Mr. Grump: Mr. Brown, nobody wants me to come to their church. I think it's best if I just stay home.

Mr. Brown: Oh Samuel . . . that's not true. Our entire church has been praying for you, by name, every Wednesday night in our prayer meeting. I know EVERYONE would be thrilled if you would come.

Mr. Grump: They would?

Mr. Brown: Yes, I know they would. Besides you need to find out the true meaning of Christmas.

(Scene changes to choir.)

Choir: "What Child Is This?"

(Scriptures to be read from whatever version your church is most familiar.)

Reader: Matthew 1:18-25

Choir: "Angels, from the Realms of Glory"

Reader: Luke 1:26-38

Choir: "Silent Night"

Reader: Luke 1:39-56

Choir: "O Holy Night!"

Reader: Luke 2:1-20

Choir: "Joy to the World"

Reader: Matthew 2:1-12

Choir: "Angels We Have Heard on High"

(Scene changes to Mr. Grump and Mr. Brown.)

Mr. Grump: Mr. Brown, I really want to thank you for bringing me to your Christmas program tonight.

Mr. Brown: Oh Samuel, you are more than welcome. I hope you were able to understand the true message our young people were trying to get across.

Mr. Grump: Oh Mr. Brown, it brought back so many memories of when I was just a young fellow. Of the times that my dear Mama read to me the "Christmas Story" from the Bible. I've been so wrong Mr. Brown. I am just an old sinner. I don't think there is any hope for me.

Mr. Brown: Nonsense Samuel. There is hope for you. God is there for you. Tell Him you believe in Him. Tell Him you have sinned and you are sorry and now you want to obey and follow Him. Ask Him to forgive you. Let's pray about it right now.

Choir: "What Child Is This?" *(chorus only)*

Christmas Questions

Dixie Phillips

Assign an older child to ask the questions. Dress the children in biblical costumes to match the Christmas characters they answer for.

Older Child: What did the angels say on that Christmas Day?

Angel (s): Glory to God in the highest!

Older Child: What did the shepherds say on that Christmas Day?

Shepherd (s): We heard angels sing about a newborn King.

Older Child: What did the wise men say on that Christmas Day?

Wise Men: We saw a star shining from afar.

Older Child: What did the innkeeper say on that Christmas Day?

Innkeeper: I have no room for you today.

Older Child: What do we say on this Christmas Day?

Unison: Come to my heart, Lord Jesus, there's room in my heart for You!